Contents

Words in bold, **like this**, are explained in the Glossary.

Introducing the Mississippi River

The mighty Mississippi

The Mississippi River carries more water than any other river in North America. It stretches from north to south, right across the USA, for a total distance of 2350 miles (3780 kilometres). If its major **tributary**, the Missouri River, is included, then the Mississippi–Missouri river system is the fourth longest in the world at 3710 miles (5970 kilometres). Besides being one of the USA's main geographical features, the Mississippi has also played a central role in the history of the USA.

This hut is a recreation of the type of river dwellings that were built on the Mississippi by Native Americans.

River glossary

Confluence – *the point where two rivers join.*

Delta – *where the river joins the sea.*

Mouth – *the ending point of a river.*

Reaches – *used to describe sections of the river (upper, middle and lower reaches).*

River course – *the path followed by a river from source to mouth.*

Source – *the starting point of a river.*

Tributary – *a river or stream that joins another (normally bigger) river.*

JGH TIME

s of the

SIPPI
River

Rob Bowden

www.heinemann.co.uk/library
Visit our website to find out more information about **Heinemann Library** books.

To order:
☎ Phone 44 (0) 1865 888066
🖹 Send a fax to 44 (0) 1865 314091
💻 Visit the Heinemann Bookshop at www.heinemann.co.uk/library to browse our catalogue and order online.

First published in Great Britain by Heinemann Library, Halley Court, Jordan Hill, Oxford OX2 8EJ, part of Harcourt Education. Heinemann is a registered trademark of Harcourt Education Ltd.

© Harcourt Education Ltd 2005.
First published in paperback in 2006.
The moral right of the proprietor has been asserted.

Editorial: Jilly Attwood and Kate Bellamy
Design: Richard Parker and
    Tinstar Design Ltd (www.tinstar.co.uk)
Illustrator: Stephen Sweet (pp. 7, 10, 16, 24, 30, 36)
    Jeff Edwards (pp. 25, 34, 38, 40, 42)
Picture Research: Ginny Stroud-Lewis
Production: Séverine Ribierre
Originated by Dot Gradations Ltd
Printed in China by WKT Company Lmited

ISBN 0 431 12045 5 (hardback)
09 08 07 06 05
10 9 8 7 6 5 4 3 2 1

ISBN 0 431 12050 1 (paperback)
10 09 08 07 06
10 9 8 7 6 5 4 3 2 1

British Library Cataloguing in Publication Data
Bowden, Rob
Settlements of the Mississippi River – (Rivers through time)
976.2
A full catalogue record for this book is available from the British Library.

Acknowledgements
The publishers would like to thank the following for permission to reproduce photographs:
Alamy p. 14; Corbis pp. 13, 18, 19, 26; Corbis pp. 21, 27, 28, 31, 32 (Bettman), 33 (Kevin Fleming), 20 (the Mariners Museum), 35 (Buddy Mays), 39 (Bill Ross); Eye Ubiquitous pp. 5, 8, 17; Hutchison p. 22; Lonely Planet p. 13; Minnesota Historical Society p. 39, 41; National Park Services p. 11; North Winds Picture Archive pp. 4, 9; Pictures Colour Library pp. 23, 29, 43

Cover photograph reproduced with permission of Lonely Planet Images.

Archaeological evidence shows that Native Americans lived alongside the Mississippi as far back as 12,000 years ago. All that remains of these ancient **settlements** are earthen mounds which have led to the Native Americans being known as 'the mound builders'. Some mounds would have been the base for important buildings such as chiefs' houses or **shrines**. Others were burial mounds.

Early, and more recent, settlers would have been attracted to the river for similar reasons. With no roads or railways, the river was the quickest way to travel and the best way to transport goods for **trade** between settlements. The Mississippi also provided fish, and its fertile **floodplains** were good for farming.

Today, the Mississippi is one of the busiest rivers in the world and one of the USA's major transportation routes. It also provides water to some of America's best farmland and to many of its biggest cities, including Minneapolis and St Louis. The Mississippi has also become a centre of American **culture**, with Blues music and rock and roll from Memphis, and jazz music and the world-famous **Mardi Gras** carnival in New Orleans.

Tow barges transport cargo along the Mississippi River – one of the world's busiest waterways.

5

The Mississippi from source to mouth

The source of the Mississippi is in the state of Minnesota, close to the border with Canada. It emerges from Lake Itasca at a relatively low **altitude** of just 450 metres. Lake Itasca itself is a clear, shallow lake, surrounded by pine forests. It was named Itasca by the explorer Henry Rowe Schoolcraft in 1832. It comes from the Latin words *veritas caput*, which mean 'true head' – referring to the source or 'head' of the river. The waters leave Lake Itasca over a line of submerged boulders. Many tourists visit this spot to walk across the waters of the Mississippi as it begins its long journey south to the Gulf of Mexico.

In its upper **reaches**, the young Mississippi flows through a marshy area of numerous small lakes and streams. There are few settlements here, but it is popular with tourists for walking, fishing and camping. There are also reserves for Native American groups such as the Ojibwe, who still live near the source of the Mississippi. In the twin cities of Minneapolis and St Paul the Mississippi flows over St Anthony's Falls. This is the only set of waterfalls on the entire river. Downstream of the waterfalls the Mississippi widens and becomes properly **navigable**. Between here and St Louis (a distance of around 1080 kilometres or 670 miles) the river is joined by most of its major tributaries, including the Minnesota, Wisconsin, Illinois and Missouri rivers.

The middle reaches of the Mississippi stretch for around 330 kilometres (200 miles) between St Louis and the river's **confluence** with the Ohio River in Cairo. It flows much faster in this section and becomes murky brown in colour after being joined by the River Missouri just north of St Louis. The colour is caused by large quantities of **silt** that are carried by the Missouri River. They give the Missouri its other name, 'the big muddy'. After the confluence with the Ohio River, the Mississippi slows and widens as it enters its long lower reaches. The river is now 2.5 kilometres (1.5 miles) wide in places and begins to **meander** wildly from side to side, sometimes almost going back on itself.

The Mississippi is joined by many more tributaries before it finally enters the swamps and **bayous** around New Orleans. This is the Mississippi **delta**, a giant wetland where the river slows and deposits its silt before finally joining the Gulf of Mexico.

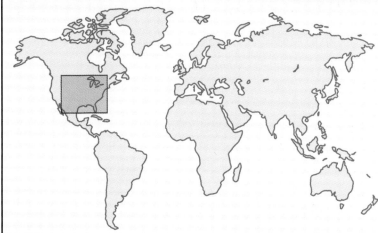

Map of the Mississippi River from its source at Lake Itasca to its mouth at the Gulf of Mexico.

MINNESOTA
Lake Itasca

CANADA

UNITED STATES
OF AMERICA

Minneapolis

St. Paul

WISCONSIN

Madison

Rocky
Mountains

New York

Missouri River

IOWA

Des Moines

Mississippi River

Illinois River

INDIANA

OHIO

ILLINOIS

Indianapolis

WEST
VIRGINIA

Springfield

Ohio River

KEY
● Case study location
● State capital
 River
 National border
 State border

Jefferson City

St. Louis

Appalachian Mountains

MISSOURI

KENTUCKY

N
W—E
S

0   Miles   300
0 Kilometres 500

ARKANSAS
Arkansas River

Mississippi River

Nashville

TENNESSEE

Memphis

Little Rock

MISSISSIPPI

ALABAMA

ATLANTIC
OCEAN

LOUISIANA

Jackson

MEXICO

Baton Rouge

New Orleans

FLORIDA

Mississippi Delta

GULF OF MEXICO

Settlements of the Mississippi

The Mississippi does not run through any mountains or high ground, so people have been able to settle along almost its entire length. Many of these settlements are just small farming communities. People have settled here to take advantage of the fertile floodplains of the Mississippi. These provide some of the best farmland in the USA and are one of the most heavily farmed areas in the world. The major crops include **maize**, cotton and sugar. The Mississippi is central to the farming industry. It provides water for **irrigation**, but more importantly it is a transportation route for taking produce to other parts of the USA or abroad. In 2003 almost half of the USA's grain exports were transported down the Mississippi.

What's in a name?

The name 'Mississippi' originates with the Dakota tribe of Native Americans, who once lived in the area north of St Louis. They referred to the river as the 'Father of Waters'. In their language this was said as Misi *meaning 'big' and* Sipi *meaning 'water'.*

The land surrounding the Mississippi is some of the most important farmland in the USA.

Paddle-wheel steamboats brought big changes to the Mississippi and its settlements.

The combination of farming, river transport and trade has led to several settlements developing into larger towns and then cities. These are often located at important points on the river. Minneapolis and St Louis, for example, are at places where the Mississippi is joined by another river. Other settlements became important staging posts (stopping places) for the **steamboats** that revolutionized transport on the Mississippi in the 19th century. Memphis, for example, became a trading point between the important market town of St Louis and the growing ports of Baton Rouge and New Orleans.

In this book we will explore some of the best-known settlements of the Mississippi River. We will follow a passage through time, starting with Baton Rouge and ending in Minneapolis – today the biggest settlement on the Mississippi. We will look at why each settlement was founded in its particular location, and at how they changed over time. What are they like today and how might they change in the future? Most importantly, we will discover how the settlements are linked to the Mississippi and to the lives of the people living there. This will show us how the importance of the Mississippi and the surrounding area has changed over time.

Baton Rouge: ancient mounds and oil

The red stick

The first European to discover the Mississippi River was the Spanish explorer and conquistador Hernando de Soto. His expedition to explore what is now the southern USA began in 1538. In 1541 he found the Mississippi, but, sick with fever, he died on its banks in early 1542. Although de Soto made the discovery of the Mississippi for the Spanish, French explorers founded many of the first **settlements** along it.

In 1699 Pierre Le Moyne d'Iberville, a French-Canadian naval captain, sailed up the Mississippi to secure the **territory of Louisiana,** which was controlled by the French. D'Iberville noticed a red stick standing some 9 metres high on a hill to one side of the river. The stick had fish heads and bear bones attached to it and looked as though it had been part of a Native American ceremony. It is now thought that the post was a boundary marker between the Houma and the Bayougoula Indians. D'Iberville named the location after this marker, which in French was *baton* (meaning 'stick') *rouge* (meaning 'red').

The red stick was a useful marker of the first point at which high ground was found when sailing upstream from the coast. This made it an obvious place to build a settlement. The high ground provided protection from flooding and a good defensive position from any form of attack. Despite these obvious advantages, early French settlements were rather temporary, though they did build a fort there in 1719.

Four nations fought over Baton Rouge in the 18th century because of its location on the Mississippi.

ARKANSAS

MISSISSIPPI

LOUISIANA

Jackson

ALABAMA

TEXAS

Baton Rouge

Mississippi River

New Orleans

Mississippi Delta

GULF OF MEXICO

Mound builders

A series of mounds located in Baton Rouge provide evidence of early Native American settlements along the Mississippi. The mounds are believed to date back around 5000 years. The mounds may have been burial mounds or platforms for ceremonies. They may have been places where people met to go hunting and gathering. Whatever their true purpose, they serve as a reminder to the people of Baton Rouge of their town's Native American origins.

The Native American Mound of Bear Creek in the state of Mississippi.

Baton Rouge's early development was dominated by military struggles for the Mississippi. The French, Spanish, British and Americans all wanted to gain control of the river and its valuable traffic. Between 1763 and 1810 Baton Rouge changed hands no fewer than five times. It finally became part of the United States in 1810. In that year local Americans rebelled against the Spanish rulers and claimed Baton Rouge for the West Florida Republic. Three months later the Republic became part of the USA.

Open for business

Baton Rouge began to grow in size and prosperity. This was due to the arrival of paddle-wheel **steamboats**, bringing **trade** in animal skins or timber, and later in farming produce. The first steamboat to pull into Baton Rouge, the *New Orleans*, arrived in 1812. Within just ten years, river traffic increased dramatically. Baton Rouge was visited by 83 steamboats, 174 **barges** and 441 **flatboats** in 1822. The trade attracted many businesses to Baton Rouge, all of which were dependent on the river.

Changing times

Baton Rouge's **economy** received a boost when the government decided to build an army post in the town. The Pentagon Barracks were built in 1819 to defend the Mississippi River from any future attacks. The soldiers stationed there increased the demand for local goods and services. In 1820 a ferry service across the Mississippi began, allowing trade across the river. The town developed rapidly and by 1840 its population had grown to 2269. The riverfront was still the centre of activity and the **wharves** bustled with river traffic, trading cotton, sugar and at that time, slaves too. By 1860 the town's population had doubled to 5428. It now had coffee houses, a foundry and a prison. Most importantly, though, Baton Rouge had become the state capital of Louisiana – a role it continues to play today.

In 1862 Baton Rouge was badly damaged during the **American Civil War**, when it was the scene of several skirmishes (small fights) between the Union and Confederate forces. Union forces made the first move when they sailed their gunboats up the Mississippi from New Orleans. They initially took the town with little struggle, but on 5 August 1862 Confederate forces launched an attack to recapture the town.

Slavery

One of the more troubling episodes in the history of the Mississippi is the role it played in slavery. Thousands of slaves, most of them from Africa, were traded up and down the river. In 1860, slaves made up around a quarter of the population of Baton Rouge. Disagreement over whether it was right to keep slaves was one of the major causes of the American Civil War (1861–65). The Confederates supported slavery, the Union wanted it abolished. When the Union forces claimed Baton Rouge in 1862, many freed slaves flocked to the city and by 1865 African-Americans made up the majority of the population. They remained the majority until as recently as 1920.

A photo of the Pentagon Barracks during the American Civil War. The Barracks still stand on the riverfront today and are one of the oldest surviving buildings in the town.

This became known as the Battle of Baton Rouge. The Confederate forces drove the Union forces back as far as the river, where the Union naval fleet was moored. This river power gave the Union forces the upper hand, however. Their powerful gunboats forced the Confederates to abandon Baton Rouge and to get out of the boats' target range. Within a few hours the battle had been won by the Union, but it had been very costly. Around a third of the town had been destroyed.

It was not until the end of the Civil War that Baton Rouge began to recover. The river was key in this and steamer traffic remained the main business of the town for many years. As the town was rebuilt, several new industries were established. These included a **lumber** company, a brick-making factory and a **mill** for processing cottonseed into oil. In 1883 the railway arrived in Baton Rouge and led to a gradual expansion of port and industrial facilities along the Mississippi waterfront.

Oil wealth

The most dramatic growth of Baton Rouge came in the early 20th century. In 1909 Standard Oil, one of America's biggest oil companies, chose Baton Rouge as the location for a new oil refinery. Baton Rouge was close to the oilfields of Texas, Louisiana and Oklahoma, and the Mississippi River was deep enough at the town to receive large ocean-going oil tankers.

Oil refineries now dominate the Mississippi waterfront in Baton Rouge.

1541	1719	1812
Hernando de Soto discovers the Mississippi River.	Fort built by the French at Baton Rouge.	First steamboat arrives in Baton Rouge.

Oil spills

Tankers using the oil terminals at Baton Rouge have caused numerous oil spills in the Mississippi. These damage the natural environment of the river and can be very costly to clean up. In 1990 new laws were introduced in the USA to make sure only the newest and safest oil tankers are allowed on the Mississippi River.

Standard Oil built their own docks on the Mississippi to handle the specialist oil freight. Other industries followed Standard Oil so in the 1920s the docks were upgraded to meet their needs. Baton Rouge now has specialist dock facilities for handling goods like grain, **molasses** and timber as well as general cargo.

Baton Rouge's oil industry played a particularly important role in the Second World War (1939–45). The town's refineries provided around three-quarters of the USA's aviation (aircraft) fuel, and supplied hundreds of American aircraft involved in the war. With so much work available in the town during the 1940s, Baton Rouge's population more than trebled from around 35,000 to 125,000.

Baton Rouge remains one of the USA's most important ports today and oil continues to be its major industry.

The Mississippi is still very much the focus of its industry and economy. Oil, timber and agricultural goods are the main **commodities** passing through the port today. In the 1980s Baton Rouge began to exploit tourist interest in the history of the city and the river. Today, visitors can take a cruise in a replica Mississippi steamer or tour one of the old plantation homes that thrived during the slavery era.

The jobs created by tourism and the state government offices have all helped Baton Rouge's population to continue growing throughout the second half of the 20th century. Louisiana State University is also a major employer and its staff and students (34,000 in total) help support many local businesses. By the year 2000 the population of the **metropolitan** area had reached almost 603,000.

1819	1862	1883	1909
Pentagon Barracks are built at Baton Rouge.	Union forces claim Baton Rouge, and slaves are freed.	Railway arrives in Baton Rouge.	Standard Oil build a new refinery in Baton Rouge.

New Orleans: the Crescent City

City in a swamp

The city of New Orleans is unusually located in the middle of the Mississippi **delta**, a vast marshy swamp. It is a hot and wet environment that suffers frequent hurricanes and floods and is infested with mosquitoes. There is also very little land above the level of the river. The dry land that exists is not rock but mud, deposited by the river over thousands of years. This hardly sounds like a good location for a **settlement**.

New Orleans became a settlement because it lies at the mouth of the mighty Mississippi River, which at the time was the only trade route into the heart of North America.

FACT

New Orleans has suffered damage from hurricanes. In 1794 much of the city was destroyed by a series of three hurricanes.

New Orleans' position at the mouth of the Mississippi made it a very desirable site for early settlers, despite its very hot and wet climate.

New Orleans is surrounded by the waters of the Mississippi delta. The crescent that gives the city its nickname is clearly visible.

Whoever controlled this area controlled the valuable river trade between the American interior and the rest of the world. The site of New Orleans was first spotted by French explorers as early as 1682, but there are no signs that the area was settled until 1718 when Jean-Baptiste le Moyne de Bienville, a governor of French Louisiana, laid out the early section of the city on a sharp bend in the Mississippi. The city gets its nickname of the 'Crescent City', from the crescent shape of this sharp bend.

The first settlers in New Orleans were a mixture of passing Mississippi traders, European settlers and slaves who were mostly of African origin. A census in 1721 recorded that there were 470 people living in New Orleans. In the following year New Orleans was declared the capital of the French **territory of Louisiana**. Despite great optimism from the French, New Orleans grew only slowly at first. This was because there was little of value in the local area that could be traded. European ships were reluctant to visit unless they could fill their holds with worthwhile cargoes for the journey home. The French tried to encourage investment in New Orleans, but this failed causing problems in France as well as New Orleans. By the middle of the 18th century New Orleans had become a financial burden on the French state. In 1763 France gave New Orleans and Louisiana west of the Mississippi to the Spanish. The rest of Louisiana went to the British, who defeated France in the Seven Years War (1756–63).

The city awakens

Under Spanish control, New Orleans began to prosper. As it did it attracted new settlers and by the turn of the century the population had grown to around 8000 people. The city's growth was due to its location at the mouth of the Mississippi. By 1800 New Orleans had become an important storage and shipping centre. It handled sugar and rice grown locally, and cotton, wheat, timber and other goods from further upstream. From New Orleans **commodities** were loaded onto larger ocean-going ships heading for Europe or the east coast of the newly formed USA (1789). Manufactured goods also came through New Orleans from Europe, making their way up the Mississippi to Baton Rouge and St Louis.

In 1800 New Orleans passed back into the control of the French, but only for a short time. In 1803 it was sold, along with the rest of Louisiana, to the USA in a deal known as the **Louisiana Purchase**.

In 1815, US forces successfully fought off the British, who were attempting to take control of New Orleans.

18

Mississippi flatboats

*Mississippi **flatboats** were a common sight in the early days of New Orleans. These large wooden rafts were made upstream of New Orleans, loaded with grain from Missouri or Illinois and then guided downstream by teams of boatmen with long poles. Among the many hazards they might face on the way were floods, alligators, and even pirates trying to steal their cargo. When they reached New Orleans they would sell their cargo to the traders in the city. They even sold the wood that their rafts were made of because the river current was too powerful to make the return journey. Instead, the flatboat crew would begin the long walk home – a journey that could take up to three months.*

Soon after the Americans gained New Orleans, they had to defend it from a British naval attack. In 1812 the USA declared war on Great Britain over the control of highly valuable shipping routes across the Atlantic. New Orleans was an important target for the British armed forces because whoever ruled New Orleans would have control of the Mississippi and its river trade. When the British attacked in January 1815, US forces and local volunteers were ready for them. They launched a barrage of artillery and musket fire, killing the British commander and forcing the British to retreat. New Orleans was saved for the Americans. The Battle of New Orleans need never have happened, however, for just a few days earlier the British and Americans had signed a peace agreement in Belgium.

The boom years

With the introduction of the steamboat in 1812, a new and efficient form of transport, New Orleans soon became a wealthy town. Improvements in cotton farming had led to an expansion of cotton plantations along the Mississippi, so millions of bales of cotton began to be transported by steamboat to New Orleans. From there they were reloaded onto ocean-going ships for the onward journey to the **textile mills** of Great Britain.

The boom in river transport led to a massive demand for labour. Thousands of people were needed to load and unload the river boats and work in the warehouses. Jobs were also created

FACT

By 1840 New Orleans was considered to be the fourth most important port in the whole world!

Mississippi steamboats line the waterfront in New Orleans. The steamboat brought great wealth to the city.

to provide housing, food, clothing and even entertainment for the river workers and their families. Many of those who came to work in the warehouses were **immigrants** from Ireland, Germany, Great Britain, Spain and Italy, as well as from elsewhere in the USA. Thousands of slaves were imported to meet the labour demand. The population of the city grew from 8000 in 1803 to almost 170,000 by 1860.

Many new neighbourhoods were built to house the growing population, which were known as 'faubourgs' (suburbs) in New Orleans. Faubourg Sainte Marie developed as a mainly American neighbourhood, whilst Faubourg Tremé was a neighbourhood where freed African slaves lived. One of New Orleans' biggest problems was frequent flooding caused by the Mississippi or heavy rains, which are common in New Orleans. Artificial embankments called **levees** were built along the banks of the Mississippi to prevent the river from flooding onto the settlements below them. They did not always work, however, and New Orleans has been flooded several times when the levees have failed to hold back the Mississippi. Much of New Orleans still lies below the level of the Mississippi and is protected by levees.

The aftermath of serious flooding along the Mississippi, with houses and other property destroyed.

21

Changing fortunes

Following the **American Civil War** (1861–65), New Orleans continued to grow but faced several problems. Cotton production had been badly disrupted by the Civil War and factories in Great Britain began buying their cotton elsewhere. Goods that had once been transported down the Mississippi to New Orleans started being taken directly by railway to east coast cities and ports such as New York. In the early 20th century New Orleans again began to prosper due to the development of **towboats** and river **barges**, which made river transport more competitive. One towboat could tow fifteen barges, each barge carrying as much cargo as fifteen rail cars. This made Mississippi towboats the most efficient way of transporting bulky cargoes such as **petroleum**, coal, steel, sand, grain and **minerals**. The oil industry also brought a boost to New Orleans from the 1950s.

This causeway over Lake Pontchartrain provides a vital road link for New Orleans. It is one of the longest causeways in the world.

1682	1718
French explorers discover the site that becomes New Orleans.	Jean-Baptiste le Moyne de Bienville plans New Orleans.

emerged from the musical traditions of the African-Americans living in New Orleans. The world famous jazz musician Louis Armstrong was born in New Orleans in 1901, and spent his early career playing the cornet in the dance bands of Mississippi River boats.

Creole and Cajun food also emerged from New Orleans. These developed over the years from a mix of cooking traditions that include Native American, French, Spanish and African recipes. The most famous dishes are gumbo and jambalaya.

Petrochemical plants and refineries were established along the Mississippi, north of New Orleans, and the city became a centre for exploring the oil reserves beneath the Mississippi delta.

Culture and tourism

New Orleans is among America's most historically important cities. The city has created its own culture and is famous as the birthplace of jazz music in the early 1900s. This

This combination of history, music and food have turned New Orleans into a major tourist destination, and the Mississippi is important for this growing industry. Replica steamboats take passengers on cruises up the Mississippi, tracing the path of explorers who ventured upriver some 300 years ago and founded New Orleans. As then, the river remains the reason for the very existence of New Orleans, a true city of the Mississippi.

1763	1803	1900s
France gives New Orleans to the Spanish.	New Orleans is bought by the USA in the Louisiana Purchase.	Jazz music begins to develop in New Orleans.

St Louis: the Gateway City

A trade post

St Louis is located roughly halfway down the Mississippi in the state of Missouri. In 1763, two French men, Pierre Laclede and his stepson Auguste Chouteau, ventured up the Mississippi in search of a suitable location for a trading post for their fur-trade company. The land that later became St Louis was ideal. It had good access to the river and was protected from flooding by a natural hill on the riverbank. It was also just 16 kilometres (10 miles) south of the Mississippi River's **confluence** with the Missouri River, the main **tributary** of the Mississippi, providing opportunities to trade along both the Missouri and the Mississippi rivers.

In 1764 Laclede and Chouteau returned to the location and founded St Louis, named after the former King of France, Louis IX, who had become a saint in 1297. The early settlement consisted of little more than wooden buildings and a small fur-trading community. Most of the early trade was with the Native Americans of the Missouri River.

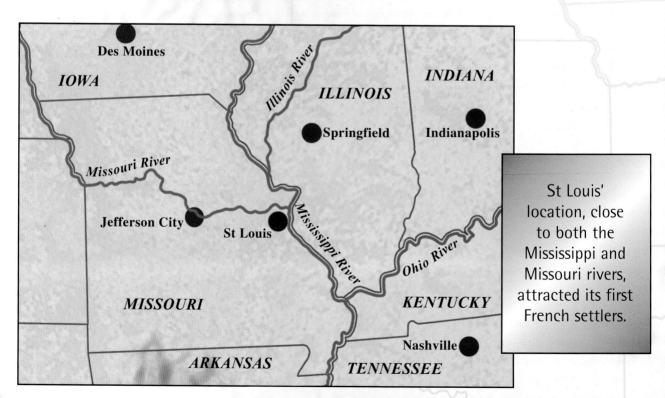

St Louis' location, close to both the Mississippi and Missouri rivers, attracted its first French settlers.

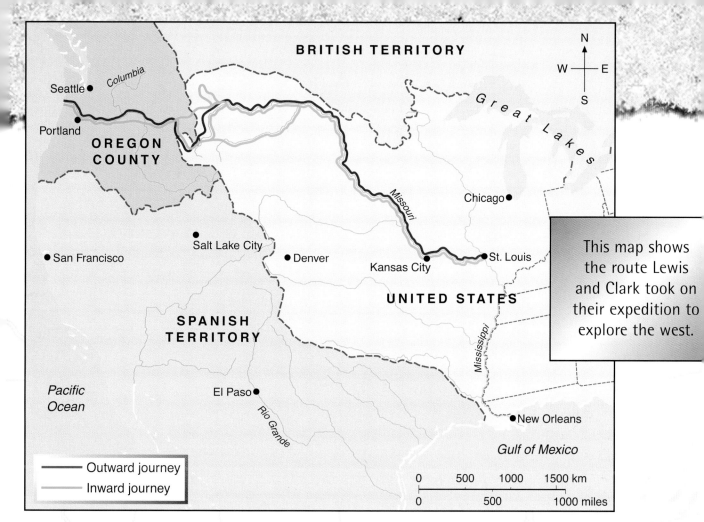

This map shows the route Lewis and Clark took on their expedition to explore the west.

Early settlers relied on supplies being brought by boat up the Mississippi, but soon St Louis established itself as an important centre for north–south trade along the Mississippi. By 1800 it had a bustling waterfront and a permanent population of around a thousand people. It soon had boat-makers, general stores, and cargo warehouses, but the fur trade continued to dominate the **economy**.

Gateway to the west

Following the **Louisiana Purchase** of 1803, St Louis became part of the USA. The following year Meriwether Lewis and William Clark were sent by President Thomas Jefferson to explore the new territories of the Louisiana Purchase. They chose St Louis as the starting point for this famous exploration of western America, which was virtually unknown to the Europeans and Americans. After gathering supplies in St Louis, Lewis and Clark headed west along the Missouri River on 14 May 1804. They did not return to St Louis until 23 September 1806, but when they did, there was much celebration and excitement. They had opened the way for the exploration of western America and helped to launch St Louis as the starting point for the long trek west where provisions and equipment could be gathered. This is why St Louis became known as the 'Gateway City'.

The age of the steamboat

Steamboats arrived in St Louis in 1817 and dominated the city for the next 60 years. The riverfront in St Louis was modified to allow the new steamboats to dock. Earthen **levees** were replaced with stone **wharves,** and warehouses were built to handle the increase in goods being transported by river. In 1849 St Louis suffered a setback when a steamer exploded and started a fire. Because most of St Louis' buildings were made of timber, the fire spread very quickly and destroyed a large part of the city.

St Louis was rebuilt using stone and iron. The river played an important role in the rebuilding. Steamboats brought iron ore upstream from mines around 100 kilometres (60 miles) south of St Louis. The river trade also provided funds for the rebuilding effort. By the mid-1850s the city was thriving again. Steamboats were sometimes lined three-deep along the city's riverfront, and St Louis became one of America's most important ports.

Many of St Louis' buildings, which were made of wood, were destroyed in a fire in 1849.

Mississippi earthquakes

On 7 February, 1812, St Louis was rocked by one of several earthquakes that occurred in the Mississippi valley at that time. The earthquake was one of the biggest in US history. The force of the earthquake flattened several houses and damaged many others. In some places the Mississippi's course was changed. Small boats were destroyed or washed onto dry land. In other areas riverbanks collapsed into the water and caused local flooding. Eyewitnesses even reported that for a short time the river flowed backwards! Thankfully, only one person was killed in the earthquake. A similar earthquake would now cost many lives and cause billions of dollars of damage.

The use of iron in St Louis became especially important at the start of the **American Civil War** in 1861. A St Louis businessman called James Eads realized that control of the Mississippi and its trade would be vital to the outcome of the war. He convinced the government to make a fleet of iron-clad steamboats to defend the river. These became known as 'the iron ships of St Louis'. They played a major part in helping Union forces capture and defend several Mississippi settlements. After the war, Eads went on to build the first railway bridge across the Mississippi at St Louis.

Eads Bridge in St Louis was opened in 1874. It was the world's first steel-truss span and is still in use today. It is a national historic landmark.

Decline and revival

The arrival of the railway signalled a change in the fortunes of St Louis. It gave the city major transport connections in all directions. The river could handle goods travelling north and south whilst the new railway connection across the Mississippi allowed goods to travel east and west. In the 1880s the use of steamboats began to decline. The railway network expanded rapidly, revolutionizing transport in the USA. By the 1920s the railway had replaced much of the river trade. River transport began to recover, however, as **towboats** and **barges** replaced the steamers. During the 20th century the port facilities in St Louis expanded into a giant complex.

In 1904 St Louis held a world's fair to celebrate the 100th anniversary of the Louisiana Purchase. More than 20 million people visited St Louis from over 40 countries. It is the biggest event ever recorded in the history of St Louis.

1763	1803	1804
Pierre Laclede and August Chouteau discover the site that becomes St Louis.	St Louis becomes part of the USA.	Expedition to explore western America sets off from St Louis.

The Gateway Arch stands as a monument to America's early pioneers.

Today the port stretches for an incredible 115 kilometres (70 miles) along both sides of the Mississippi. There are 134 piers, wharves and docks as well as 55 fleeting areas (places where fleets of barges can tie up while waiting for towboats). The main cargoes passing through St Louis today are **petroleum,** chemicals, coal and grain.

The population of the city and its suburbs is now around 2.1 million. In the second half of the 20th century the city-centre riverfront was redeveloped. One of the greatest achievements was the Gateway Arch, a steel arch standing 192 metres high, which reminds visitors about the pioneers who set out from this historic gateway to the west.

Revolutions in transport

In the early 1900s St Louis became a centre of car and aircraft manufacture. The motor car industry developed from the wagons that had been built in St Louis for the pioneers. Between 1900 and 1930 there were over 200 car manufacturers based in the city and the city remains a major car manufacturer.

Charles Lindberg, the first person to fly non-stop across the Atlantic Ocean in 1927, was sponsored by businessmen from St Louis and named his plane The Spirit of St Louis. In 1939 James McDonnell set up a factory to make fighter aircraft for the Second World War, which later became part of Boeing, the world's largest manufacturer of commercial aircraft.

1817	1849	1874	1920s
First steamboat arrives in St Louis.	A steamer explodes and causes a large fire in St Louis.	Eads bridge opens in St Louis.	Railway replaces much of the river trade in St Louis.

Memphis: cotton and music

A Native American stronghold

The first European to see the site that became Memphis was Hernando de Soto in 1541. The land around Memphis was at this time controlled by the Chickasaw Native Americans, who lived among the forested river **bluffs** of the Mississippi. They hunted bison, deer and bears in the forest and caught fish from the Mississippi. They also grew crops such as **maize**, beans and squash (similar to pumpkin).

In the 18th century the French, Spanish, British and later the Americans, were competing for control of the Mississippi River. During this period various forts were built at what was to become Memphis, to protect river trade along the Mississippi. The city itself was not founded until the following century.

FACT

One of Memphis's founders, Andrew Jackson, went on to become the seventh president of the USA (1829–37).

Memphis was founded in 1819. Besides providing the settlement with an important trading route, the Mississippi had also flooded the region's soils with nutrients.

© Goovert - Memphis, Tenn. 1926

Workers pick cotton in the plantations that grew up around Memphis and along the Mississippi River.

In 1818 the Chickasaw passed their lands over to America, and Memphis was founded the following year by John Overton, James Winchester and Andrew Jackson on 22 May.

King Cotton

From its very beginnings Memphis was an important market town and trading post. This was due to its location on one of the busiest trade routes in the country between St Louis (upstream) and New Orleans (downstream). German and Irish **immigrants** established many of the early businesses and built some of the city's oldest buildings. Memphis grew in importance thanks to cotton, sometimes referred to as 'white gold'. The countryside around Memphis was ideal for growing cotton as it had particularly rich soils. These had been deposited over thousands of years by the Mississippi in flood. As the waters receded they left behind soils rich in **minerals** and nutrients. The climate around Memphis was also suited to cotton, with warm summers and plentiful rain.

For the cotton industry, Memphis's greatest asset was its location on the Mississippi River. This made it easy to transport cotton to Europe and the more industrialized states of the northern and eastern USA. The **steamboat** was the main mode of transport at this time and Memphis soon developed a busy waterfront. By the middle of the 19th century Memphis had become the cotton capital of the mid-south. In fact it was so famous as a cotton centre that it became known as 'King Cotton'.

City of slaves

Memphis owed much of its early growth and prosperity to slavery. Thousands of slaves were brought to the city to work on the labour-intensive cotton plantations. Most of them originated from West African countries, where they were captured and sold to slave dealers. They were then shipped across the Atlantic Ocean and up the Mississippi River to be sold to plantation-owners as cotton-pickers or housekeepers. Conditions for the slaves were extremely difficult and many of them did not even survive the crossing. Those that did were bought and sold in auctions like cattle at a livestock market.

During the **American Civil War**, Memphis was largely unaffected and continued to grow. There was, however, one river battle in June 1862, when the iron-clad gunboats of the Union fleet took Memphis from the Confederates. It is said that 10,000 people lined the hills along the Mississippi to watch the battle for Memphis. The end of the Civil War also marked the end of slavery in America. Many former slaves settled in Memphis, which quickly developed into a strong black community with their own churches and neighbourhoods.

A market in Memphis sells slaves as workers for the cotton plantations.

Beale Street in Memphis is said to be the home of blues music. Its world-famous blues clubs are today a major tourist attraction.

One Memphis resident called Ed Shaw became one of the most powerful black Americans of the time. He served on the city council and was also elected **wharf** master of the riverfront. Because of the importance of the river this was a prestigious and well-paid job.

Memphis' history as a slave centre has been reflected in its culture ever since. The songs and rhythms that African slaves brought with them to Memphis led to a new form of music known as 'the blues', which developed from the 1890s onwards. Memphis was one of the most important cities for early blues music. Many of the first blues musicians played in the city and particularly on world-famous Beale Street. The Mississippi River has influenced many blues musicians to write songs about the river and the people who live and work on it. One of the most famous songs is 'Mississippi **Delta** Blues', which was written by W. C. Handy. He also wrote the songs 'Memphis Blues' and 'St Louis' Blues'.

Birthplace of rock and roll

As well as being famous as the home of the blues, Memphis is also considered to be the birthplace of rock and roll. In particular it is associated with Elvis Presley, who was influenced by blues music and lived and died in the city. He is one of the most influential musicians of all time. His home, Graceland, in Memphis, is now a museum dedicated to his life. Apart from the White House (the official residence of the US president), Graceland is the most visited house in the USA.

Trade and tourism

The Mississippi continued to be vital in the development of Memphis throughout the 20th century. Cotton still dominated its **economy** and by the mid-1900s the city traded more than 40 per cent of all cotton produced in the USA. Other important **commodities** traded in Memphis include timber, grain, **petroleum**, coal and manufactured goods. In 1946 new port facilities were built on President's Island, just downstream of the city centre, to handle the growing amount of river traffic. This used to be the biggest island in the Mississippi, but it has been connected to the mainland to protect one side of it from the risk of flooding. This sheltered side is where the new port facilities have been built.

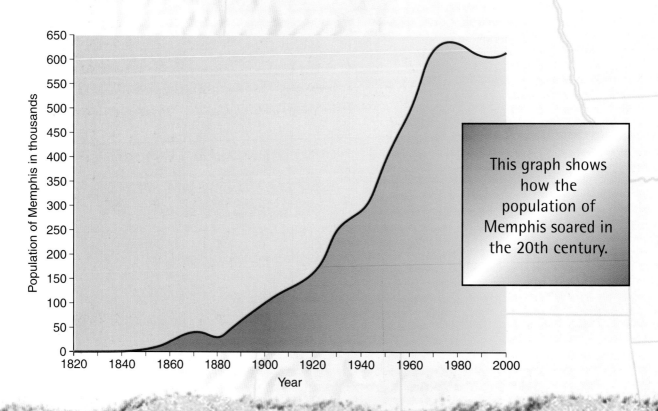

This graph shows how the population of Memphis soared in the 20th century.

1541	1818	1819
Hernando de Soto is the first European to discover the site that becomes Memphis.	The Chickasaw surrender Memphis to America.	Memphis is founded by John Overton, James Winchester and Andrew Jackson.

Cargo ships dock in Memphis' port – one of the busiest in the USA.

The port of Memphis is now one of America's leading transport and distribution centres. Each year, some 30,000 railroad cars pass through the port. The port also has connections to Memphis International Airport, which is the biggest cargo airport in the world.

Redevelopment of the city centre and waterfront began in Memphis in the 1980s to encourage more tourists to visit the city. One of the city's newest attractions is a 32-storey pyramid, which was built on the banks of the Mississippi in 1991. This unusual building is a sports and entertainments arena, but has become a popular city attraction in its own right. In May each year the Mississippi becomes the focus of a music and cultural festival called 'Memphis in May'. Many of the festival events take place in Tom Lee Park, which runs alongside the river.

The park is named after a **levee** worker who rescued 32 people from a sinking river steamer in 1925 and became a local hero.

One of Memphis' biggest tourist attractions is Mud Island River Park in the Mississippi itself. This island is home to the Mississippi River Museum, where visitors can learn about the natural and cultural history of the river. Mud Island shows that although Memphis might be changing, the river is still central to the city, its economy and its people.

FACT

The Pyramid Arena in Memphis is taller than the Statue of Liberty in New York or the Taj Mahal in India.

1946	1980s	1991
New port facilities are built in Memphis.	Redevelopment of Memphis' city centre and waterfront.	32-storey pyramid built in Memphis.

Minneapolis: the milling capital

Sacred falls

The city of Minneapolis lies at the **confluence** of the Mississippi and Minnesota rivers, and has a twin city, St Paul, located a little further to the south. It is located on land that once belonged to the Dakota tribe of Native Americas. This meeting of the rivers was considered by the Dakota to be the spiritual centre of their world. Of particular importance were a set of waterfalls on the Mississippi. The Dakota called them *Owamniyomni*, which means 'the whirlpool'. They are in fact the only natural waterfalls on the entire Mississippi River. The first European to see them was a Belgian priest called Louis Hennepin. He visited the area in the early 1680s and gave them their present name, St Anthony's Falls, after his favourite saint.

The falls were to play a crucial role in the development of Minneapolis, but it was over 200 years before any form of permanent **settlement** was established on the site. In 1805 the Dakota surrendered the land that became Minneapolis to the growing power of America. In 1819 the Americans built a fort

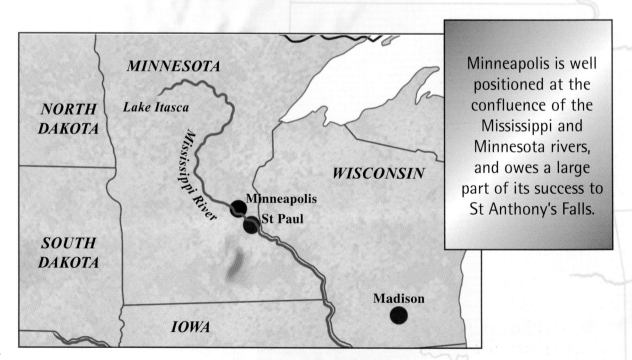

Minneapolis is well positioned at the confluence of the Mississippi and Minnesota rivers, and owes a large part of its success to St Anthony's Falls.

SEPT 16 - 1901

A view of Minneapolis in 1901. These logs are being sorted at Boom Island.

at the confluence of the Mississippi and Minnesota rivers to control the surrounding lands. The demand for timber to build the fort led to the construction of saw **mills** at St Anthony's Falls. The force of the falling water provided energy for powering the mills. The logs were brought down by river from forests located upstream. Flour mills were also constructed at the falls to help feed the fort soldiers. Both industries used the power of the Mississippi and caused the foundation of Minneapolis.

The first settlement was the small village of St Anthony on the eastern side of the Mississippi, opposite the present-day city of Minneapolis.

The settlers arrived there in the late 1840s and the settlement became a city in 1855. In the same year it was also connected to Minneapolis by a suspension bridge across the river. Minneapolis itself was first settled and named in 1852. The name comes from the Dakota word *minnehaha*, meaning 'laughing waters', and *polis*, which is Greek for 'city'. The idea for the name came from a schoolmaster called Charles Hoag who wrote to the local paper with the proposed name. It was widely welcomed and quickly adopted. In 1872 the settlement of St Anthony was merged to become part of Minneapolis. Old St Anthony remains a neighbourhood of the city today.

Milling capital of the world

Minneapolis soon began to thrive, thanks to its unique position alongside St Anthony's Falls. The water was taken from above the falls by a system of canals. The energy of the falling water was used to turn waterwheels and generate power, then the water was returned to the river downstream of the falls. Minneapolis grew rapidly as sawmills and flour mills came to take advantage of the power provided by the falls. The Mississippi also provided the transport route for bringing raw materials (grain and logs) in and for sending finished goods (flour and timber) out again.

By 1880 Minneapolis had become the flour-milling capital of the world. It held on to this title for 50 years. The Washburn A Mill was a particular success, despite suffering an enormous explosion shortly after it was built in 1874. It was the most technologically advanced mill in the world and at its peak could grind enough flour in a single day to bake 12 million loaves of bread! Timber production also peaked around this time and by 1889 Minneapolis was America's leading sawmill centre.

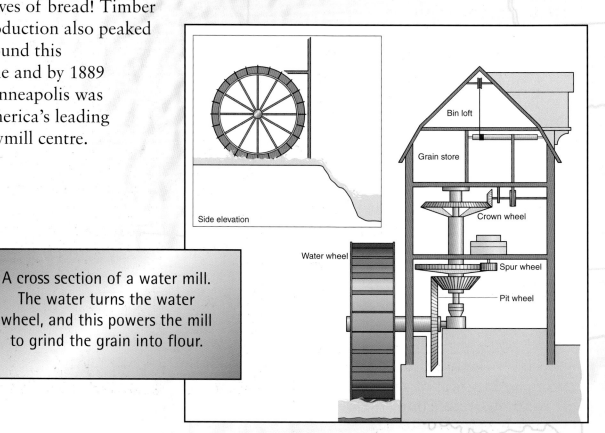

Side elevation

Bin loft

Grain store

Crown wheel

Water wheel

Spur wheel

Pit wheel

A cross section of a water mill. The water turns the water wheel, and this powers the mill to grind the grain into flour.

The population of Minneapolis grew from around 13,000 in 1870 to 165,000 by 1890. Most of the people were labourers, who came to work in the mills or industries connected to them. Towards the end of the 19th century Minneapolis' growth was boosted by the railways. Huge farms in the northwest were planted with wheat, and their harvests were transported into Minneapolis by hundreds of rail wagons.

The timber industry still relied on the Mississippi for bringing logs down to Minneapolis from the forests of the north. In 1899 so many logs were transported in this way that they completely blocked the river above Minneapolis. By 1906 Minneapolis's sawmills were in decline as the forests of the north were cleared. The last sawmill closed in 1921, but the flour mills continued until well into the 1960s.

With Minneapolis at the centre of the US grain and flour industry it became a major financial market as well as a manufacturing centre. The Minneapolis Grain Exchange was founded in 1881 and rapidly became the USA's most important grain market. Banking and insurance soon followed, to meet the demands of farmers, millers and customers. These financial industries gradually took over during the 20th century and are today the main **economic** activity in Minneapolis.

This photo, taken in 1949, shows the Pillsbury 'A' Mill in Minneapolis, one of the biggest mills on the river.

FACT

So much water was taken from the Mississippi to power the mills of Minneapolis that St Anthony's Falls were sometimes known to dry up.

Stairway of water

As the only waterfalls on the Mississippi, St Anthony's Falls created a break in the **navigation** of the Mississippi River, preventing steamboats from travelling beyond St Paul, the twin city of Minneapolis located just downstream. From there, people and goods had to transfer to land for the onward journey. The first plans to extend navigation above the falls were laid in 1850, but it would be more than 100 years before this was achieved. Early attempts to control the flow of St Anthony's Falls had ended in disaster, destroying large sections of the waterfall. It was not until 1885 that the US Army Corps of Engineers finally stabilized the falls.

Locks

A lock is a device used on rivers or canals that allows boats to be raised or lowered from one water level to another. The main feature of a lock is the chamber, which has gates that can be opened and closed at either end. The water in the chamber is controlled by opening or shutting paddles. Once the boat reaches the correct level the gates are opened for it to continue its journey either up- or downstream. This is an example of a manual lock.

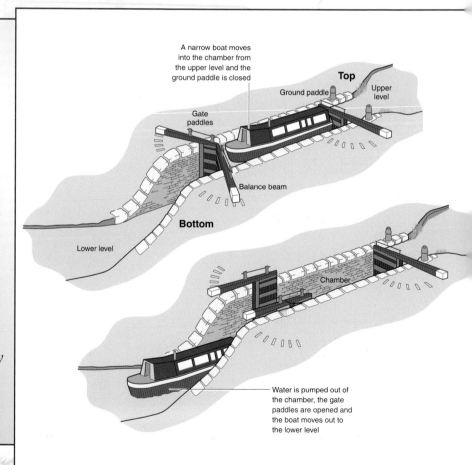

A narrow boat moves into the chamber from the upper level and the ground paddle is closed

Top

Ground paddle

Upper level

Gate paddles

Balance beam

Bottom

Lower level

Chamber

Water is pumped out of the chamber, the gate paddles are opened and the boat moves out to the lower level

1680	1819	1852
Louis Hennepin names the St Anthony's Falls at Minneapolis.	The Americans built a fort at the confluence of the Mississippi and Minnesota rivers.	Minneapolis is first settled and named.

A photo from 1954 of a ship lock being built alongside St Anthony's Falls in Minneapolis. The locks have greatly boosted river cargo on the Mississippi.

In the first half of the 20th century, navigation between Minneapolis and St Louis was improved by a series of locks and dams that were built along the Mississippi. St Anthony's Falls still presented a natural barrier, which was finally overcome in 1963, when two new locks were completed to guide river traffic above Minneapolis for the first time.

Today the locks over St Anthony's Falls are vital to the navigation of the upper Mississippi. Before they were completed, **barge** traffic on the upper Mississippi River handled around 27 million tons of cargo each year. This has now increased to around 80 million tons a year.

The locks also make it possible for pleasure craft to navigate the river and have even become a popular tourist attraction in their own right. Together with its twin city of St Paul, Minneapolis is now home to around 2.5 million people, all of whom owe their success in some way to the Mississippi. In September 2003 a new museum, The Mill City Museum, opened in Minneapolis to celebrate this fact. It acts as a reminder to future generations of the time when Minneapolis was the world's greatest mill town.

1855	1872	1881	1963
St Anthony becomes a city and is connected to Minneapolis by a suspension bridge.	St Anthony is merged to become part of Minneapolis.	Minneapolis Grain Exchange founded.	Two new locks guide traffic above Minneapolis for the first time.

The Mississippi of tomorrow

What of the future?

The Mississippi River of today would be barely recognizable to the explorers and pioneers who founded its early **settlements**. Cities such as St Louis and New Orleans that were once small trading villages are today vast cities with millions of people. One thing they would recognize, however, is the importance of the river as a major trade route. Although the type of transport and cargo seen on the Mississippi may have changed, it remains a vital waterway for the people and settlements living alongside it. But what will the future hold for the Mississippi and its settlements?

Tourism is almost certain to increase. Memphis and New Orleans are already especially popular tourist destinations, but all of the Mississippi's settlements are likely to receive more tourists. One feature that will increase tourism and bring all the settlements of the Mississippi closer together is the Mississippi River Trail.

This graphic map shows how Minneapolis has expanded since 1840.

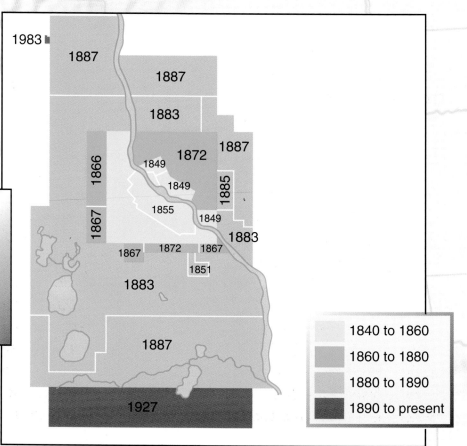

1983
1887
1887
1883
1866
1872
1849
1887
1849
1885
1867
1855
1849
1883
1867 1872 1867
1851
1883
1887
1927

1840 to 1860
1860 to 1880
1880 to 1890
1890 to present

Tourists on board a modern **steamboat** on the Mississippi River.

This will be a 3220-kilometre (2000-mile) long cycle trail that follows the Mississippi through ten states. Parts of the trail are already open, but others will be added soon. The river itself remains a major tourist attraction for river cruises or other boating activities on the Mississippi.

Living with the Mississippi

For as long as people have lived along the Mississippi they have had to cope with the risk of flooding and this continues to be the case. The last major flood on the Mississippi took place in 1993. It covered land in 9 states, damaged some 56,000 homes and killed 50 people. St Louis was under great threat during the floods, but the **levee** walls held back the waters and protected the city and its

people. Many of the levees in rural areas did not hold and others were not high enough. After the flood, repairs were needed to thousands of kilometres of levees along the Mississippi and its **tributaries**.

The 1993 flood has led to great debate about the future of the Mississippi River. Some believe that measures such as the construction of levees to protect settlements and farmland may have contributed to the flooding. Others argue that without the levees the damage would have been much greater – St Louis, for example, would have been badly flooded, causing billions of dollars of damage. In reality a river as mighty as the Mississippi is never likely to be tamed by the people living alongside it. Instead, they have to learn to live with the river – and its floods.

Timeline

6000 BC	Native Americans live along the Mississippi River.
AD 1541	Hernando de Soto discovers the Mississippi.
1682	French explorers discover the site that becomes New Orleans.
1718	Jean-Baptiste le Moyne de Bienville plans New Orleans.
1719	Fort is built by the French at Baton Rouge.
1763	France gives New Orleans to the Spanish.
1763	Pierre Laclede and August Chouteau discover the site that becomes St Louis.
1789	United States of America is formed.
1803	New Orleans is bought by the USA in the **Louisiana Purchase**.
1803	St Louis becomes part of the USA.
1804	Expedition to explore western America sets off from St Louis.
1811–1812	Several severe earthquakes occur in the Mississippi valley.
1812	First **steamboat** arrives in Baton Rouge.
1817	First steamboat arrives in St Louis.
1818	The Chickasaw surrender Memphis to America.
1819	Memphis is founded by John Overton, James Winchester and Andrew Jackson.
1819	Pentagon Barracks are built at Baton Rouge.
1832	Itasca Lake is named by explorer Henry Rowe Schoolcraft.
1849	A steamer explodes and causes a large fire in St Louis.
1862	Union forces claim Baton Rouge and slaves are freed.
1862	Battle over Memphis in the **American Civil War**.
1874	Eads Bridge opens in St Louis.
1883	Railway arrives in Baton Rouge.
1885	US Army Corps of Engineers stabilize St Anthony's Falls.
1890s	Blues music develops in Memphis.
1900s	Jazz music begins to develop in New Orleans.
1909	Standard Oil build a new refinery in Baton Rouge.
1920s	Railway replaces much of the river trade in St Louis.
1921	Last sawmill closes in Minneapolis.
1946	New port facilities are built in Memphis.
1980s	Redevelopment of Memphis city centre and waterfront.
1991	32-storey pyramid is built in Memphis.
2003	Mill City Museum opens in Minneapolis.

Further resources

Books

A River Journey: The Mississippi,
Martin Curtis and Simon Milligan (Hodder Wayland, 2003)

The Mississippi,
Michael Pollard (Evans Brothers, 1997)

The Mississippi (Rivers of the World),
Stephen Currie (Lucent Books, 2002)

Websites

American rivers
(**www.americanrivers.org**)
A site all about America's rivers that focuses especially on their conservation. Several links and articles relating to the Mississippi.

Friends of the Mississippi River
(**www.fmr.org**)
An organization that promotes the Mississippi in the area around the twin cities of Minneapolis and St Paul.

Mississippi River Parkway Commission
(**www.mississippiriverinfo.com**)
Website giving information about the Mississippi River and the Great River Road, which follows the river for its entire length.

Glossary

altitude height above sea level, measured in feet or metres

American Civil War war fought in the USA between the two rival political parties, the Confederates and the Unionists, between 1861-65

archaeology study of the past using evidence that was left behind, which usually lies buried under ground

barge narrow, long and flat bottomed boat used for transporting goods. Some barges are also used to carry people.

bayou area of slow-moving water in the southern USA. A bayou is often swampy and overgrown with water-loving plants.

bluff a steep hill, mound or cliff

commodity item that is bought and sold. Normally used to describe raw materials and farming produce.

confluence point at which two (or more) river channels meet

delta area at the mouth of a river, formed by the deposit of sand and soil in a triangular shape

economy goods and services produced and used by a community

flatboat wooden boat with a flat bottom that is directed down a river using long poles. It was common on the Mississippi River before the arrival of the steamboat in the early 19th century.

floodplain land to the side of a river that is frequently flooded during periods when the river is in full flow

immigrant person who moves into an area from somewhere outside (often another country)

irrigation watering crops using specially created systems. Normally used in areas of low rainfall.

levee artificial embankment built alongside a river channel to protect land from being flooded

Louisiana Purchase the sale of a large part of modern-day western USA from France to the newly formed US government in 1803

lumber wood taken from trees that has been sawn and prepared for use in building or manufacturing

maize cereal crop, also known as corn

Mardi Gras alternative name for Shrove Tuesday. In New Orleans this is celebrated with a major street carnival involving musicians, dancing and brightly coloured costumes.

meander wind from side to side rather than follow a direct (straight) route

metropolitan a city and its surrounding suburbs

mill building in which machinery is housed to convert raw materials into finished goods, such as grain into flour or timber into lumber

mineral substance found naturally in the ground and mined for its value. Coal, gold and iron ore are examples of minerals.

molasses syrup produced by the processing and manufacture of raw sugar

navigable stretch of water on which it is possible to travel by ship or boat

navigation act of directing or moving a boat along a river or across a lake or sea

petrochemical substance made from petroleum or natural gas such as petrol, paraffin or kerosene

petroleum crude oil that is used to make a variety of petrochemicals such as petrol and kerosene fuels

reaches part of a river's course. Rivers are normally divided into middle, upper and lower reaches.

settlement place that has people living in it permanently. Settlements can vary in size from a small village to a large city.

shrine a place of worship, normally linked to a holy site or a holy person

silt soil and gravel carried by a river and deposited as it slows down along its banks, its bottom or in its delta

steamboat (or 'steamer') boat where the engine is powered by the production of steam, normally by burning coal

territory of Louisiana area of the eastern USA and Canada that was once under the control of the French. It included, but was much bigger than, the present-day state of Louisiana.

textile manufactured cloth or fabric, made by weaving or knitting

towboat a powerful boat used to tow or push cargo barges along a river. One towboat may be able to move 15 large barges.

tributary river or stream that joins another, normally larger, river

wharf structure built alongside or into a river channel that enables boats to dock and unload their goods or passengers

Index